Busy ABC

COLIN AND JACQUI HAWKINS

Daniel is drawing Dilly.

Dolores is drinking.

Donna is dancing.

Hh

Helen is
hopping.

Harriet is hugging Harry.

Ii

Isobel is inviting
Inky and Iggy.

Jane and Jack are jumping.

Ll

Leo is looking in the mirror.

Mm

Malcolm is marching.

Maya is munching.

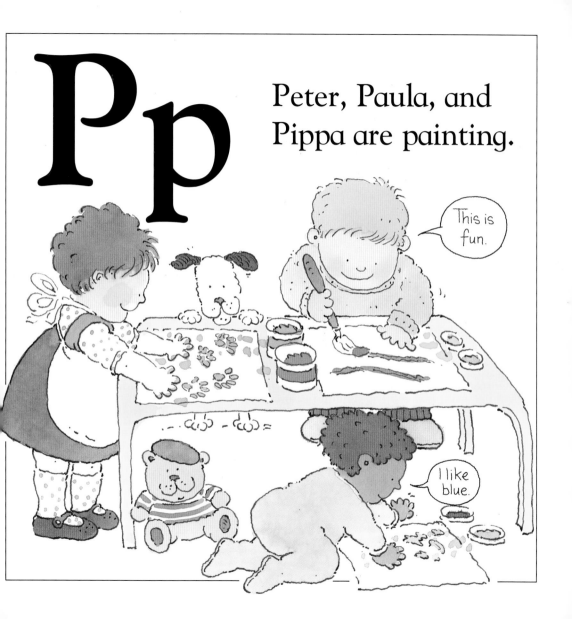

Qq

Quentin and Queenie are quarrelling.

Sophie is sliding.

Sam is sitting on the slide.

Tt

Timmy is tripping.

Uu

Unity is undressing.

Ursula is undoing her coat.

Vv

Vanessa is visiting
Victor and Valerie.

Xavier is xylophoning.

A DORLING KINDERSLEY BOOK

Published in the United Kingdom in 1996
by Dorling Kindersley Limited,
9 Henrietta Street, London WC2E 8PS
Visit us on the World Wide Web at http://www.dk.com

2 4 6 8 10 9 7 5 3

ISBN 0-7513-7033-9

Reproduction by DOT Gradations
Printed by Tien Wah Press in Singapore